AN
ILLUSTRATED
WOMAN'S
NOTEBOOK

ILLUSTRATED BY
JULIETTE CLARKE

EDITED BY
HELEN EXLEY

EXLEY
NEW YORK • WATFORD, UK

What is better than gold?
 Jasper.
What is better than jasper?
 Wisdom.
What is better than wisdom?
 Women.
And what is better than a good woman?
 Nothing.
  Geoffrey Chaucer (1340-1400)

For women there are, undoubtedly, great difficulties in the path, but so much the more to overcome. First, no woman should say, "I am but a woman!" But a woman! What more can you ask to be?

Maria Mitchell (1818-1889)

To me gender is not physical at all, but is altogether insubstantial. It is soul, perhaps, it is talent, it is taste, it is environment, it is how one feels, it is light and shade, it is inner music.

Jan Morris,
from "Conundrum"

*Traditionally we are taught, and instinctively we long, to give
where it is needed – and immediately. Eternally, woman spills
herself away in driblets to the thirsty, seldom being allowed the
time, the quiet, the peace, to let the pitcher fill up to the brim.*
Anne Morrow Lindbergh, b.1906,
from "Gift From The Sea"

In my younger days, when I was pained by the half-educated, loose and inaccurate ways women had, I used to say, "How much women need exact science." But since I have known some workers in science, I have now said, "How much science needs women."

Maria Mitchell (1818-1889)

A liberated woman is one who feels confident in herself, and is happy in what she is doing. She is a person who has a sense of self.... It all comes down to freedom of choice.

Betty Ford

Being a woman is of special interest only to aspiring male transsexuals. To actual women, it is simply a good excuse not to play football.
Fran Lebowitz, b.1961

Above the titles of wife and mother, which, although dear, are transitory and accidental, there is the title human being, which precedes and outranks every other.
                                    Mary Ashton Livermore (c.1820-1905)

It is <u>new</u> for women to be making history – not just a few queens, empresses or exceptional geniuses, but hundreds, thousands, millions of women now entering history, knowing we have made history – by changing our own lives.

Betty Friedan, b.1921,
from "It Changed My Life"

Women! There isn't anything so bad that they don't soon start to enjoy it. Even if they lived in a barrel of shit they'd start making a home of it, with everything nice and cozy.
Eeva-Lusa Manner, b.1921

*At present, we insist that a woman be treated
just the same as a man. Are we sure we want
to be treated as most men are in our society?
Or do both sexes deserve something better?*
                        *Kay Keeshan Hamod,
                        from "Working It Out"*

What a circus act we women perform every day of our lives. It puts the trapeze artist to shame. Look at us. We run a tight rope daily, balancing a pile of books on the head. Baby-carriage, parasol, kitchen chair, still under control. Steady now!

Anne Morrow Lindbergh, b.1906,
from "Gift From The Sea"

I think it is time that male leaders look to women leaders as role models. They will find that persuasion brings better results than confrontation. And, finally, they will realize that, when dealing with the nations of the world, reconciliation unites people and allows them to work together for the benefit of all.

Violeta Chamorro,
from Introduction Speech for International Hall of Fame

Women...often...need to return to their past, to the women who were part of that past, to girlhood when a self existed that was individual and singular, defined neither by men, nor children, nor home, almost as though with the layers of roles and responsibilities they have covered over a real person and must now peel back those layers and reclaim the self that was just emerging in adolescence.

Mary Helen Washington

...each woman is far from average in the daily heroics of her life, even though she may never receive a moment's recognition in history.
Introduction to "Women & Work"

Men weren't really the enemy – they were fellow victims
suffering from an outmoded masculine mystique that
made them feel unnecessarily inadequate when there were
no bears to kill.

Betty Friedan, b. 1921,
from "Christian Science Monitor"

Everything that gives birth is female. When men begin to understand the relationships of the universe that women have always known, the world will begin to change for the better.

Lorraine Canoe
(Mohawk)

*I don't believe make-up and the right
hairstyle alone can make a woman
beautiful. The most radiant woman in the
room is the one most full of life and
experience.*

Sharon Stone

All women have a sacred obligation to each other irrespective of class or conditions of work.

Vida Goldstein

I don't mind being in a man's world
so long as I can be a woman in it.
        Marilyn Monroe (1926-1962)

It would be a thousand pities if women wrote like men,
or lived like men, or looked like men, for if two sexes are
quite inadequate, considering the vastness and variety of
the world, how should we manage with one only?
                                        Virginia Woolf (1882-1941)

Being nice should <u>never</u> be perceived as being weak. It's not a sign of weakness, it's a sign of courtesy, manners, grace, a woman's ability to make everyone...feel at home, and it should never be construed as weakness....

Benazir Bhutto, b.1953

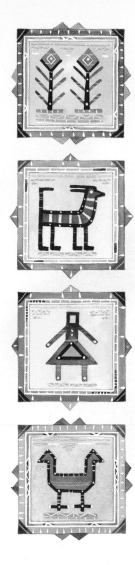

One of the wonderful things about women, which I don't think many social anthropologists have fully understood, is that we are bonded by shared experiences....

Anita Roddick, b.1943,
from "Body and Soul"

Woman must be still as the axis of a wheel in the midst of her activities; ...she must be the pioneer in achieving this stillness, not only for her own salvation, but for the salvation of family life, of society, perhaps even of our civilization.

Anne Morrow Lindbergh, b.1906
from "Gift From The Sea"

*I think the key is for women
not to set any limits.*
  Martina Navratilova, b.1956

Very often, men are pursuing some fantasy of school, or their fathers, or their nation. Women are slightly more rooted in themselves. That's not to say they're more introspective, but they just have a presence; they've had to.

Joan Bakewell, b.1933

Womankind holds at its heart the understanding that love, not power, ensures the continuance of life. Each woman holds the hope of reconciliation, of sanity, of peace, of strength in kindness, of humankind discovering it is one family.

Pam Brown, b.1928

Women never have an half-hour in all their lives (excepting before or after anybody is up in the house) that they can call their own, without fear of offending or of hurting someone. Why do people sit up so late, or, more rarely, get up so early? Not because the day is not long enough, but because they have "no time in the day to themselves."

Florence Nightingale (1820-1910), from "Cassandra"

I believe that what a woman resents is not so much giving herself in pieces as giving herself purposelessly.

Anne Morrow Lindbergh, b.1906

The great and almost only comfort about being a woman is that one can always pretend to be more stupid than one is and no one is surprised.

Freya Stark (1893-1993)

We women suffragists have a great mission – the greatest mission the world has ever known. It is to free half the human race, and through that reason to save the rest.

Emmeline Pankhurst (1857-1928)

Religion, science, art, economics, have all needed the feminine flavor; and literature, the expression of what is permanent and best in all of these, may be gauged by any time to measure the strength of the feminine ingredient.

Anna Julia Cooper

The Golden Rule works for men as written, but for women it should go the other way around. We need to do unto ourselves as we do unto others.
Gloria Steinem, b.1934

For the sake of the sons - and even for the sons' future wives - a woman must keep a part of her mind and heart entirely for herself. Every family is better off with a wife and mother who can astonish and occasionally bewilder.

Pam Brown, b.1928

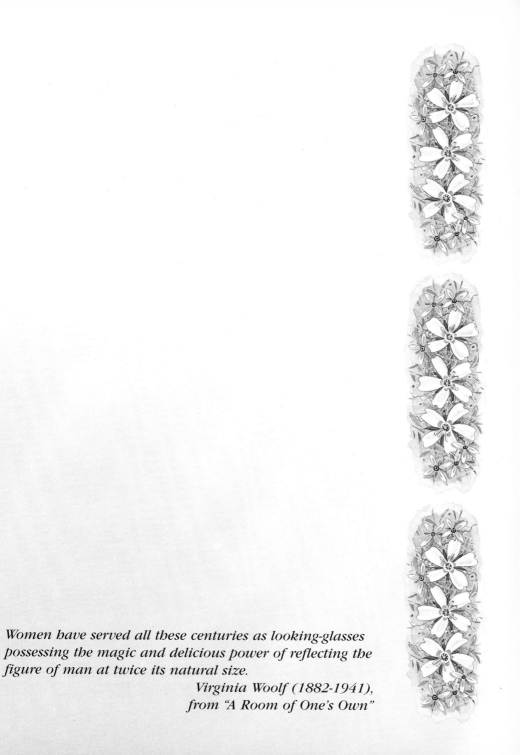

Women have served all these centuries as looking-glasses
possessing the magic and delicious power of reflecting the
figure of man at twice its natural size.

Virginia Woolf (1882-1941),
from "A Room of One's Own"

*Women speak because they wish to speak,
whereas a man speaks only when driven to
speech by something outside himself – like, for
instance, he can't find any clean socks.*

Jean Kerr

Nothing on Earth is more gladdening than knowing we must roll up our sleeves and move back the boundaries of the humanly possible once more.

Annie Dillard

The people I'm furious with are the women's liberationists. They keep getting up on soap boxes and proclaiming that women are brighter than men. It's true but it should be kept quiet or it ruins the whole racket.

Anita Loos, b.1893,
from "International Herald Tribune" 1973

Even today when we extol the virtues of our mamas, most often it's a litany of hard work, of what she did without and what she gave – never what she took or expected or demanded as her due.

Marcia Ann Gillespie

Woman's life today is tending more and more toward the state William James describes so well in the German word, "Zerrissenheit – torn-to-pieces-hood." She cannot live perpetually in "Zerrissenheit." She will be shattered into a thousand pieces.

Anne Morrow Lindbergh, b.1906
from "Gift From The Sea"

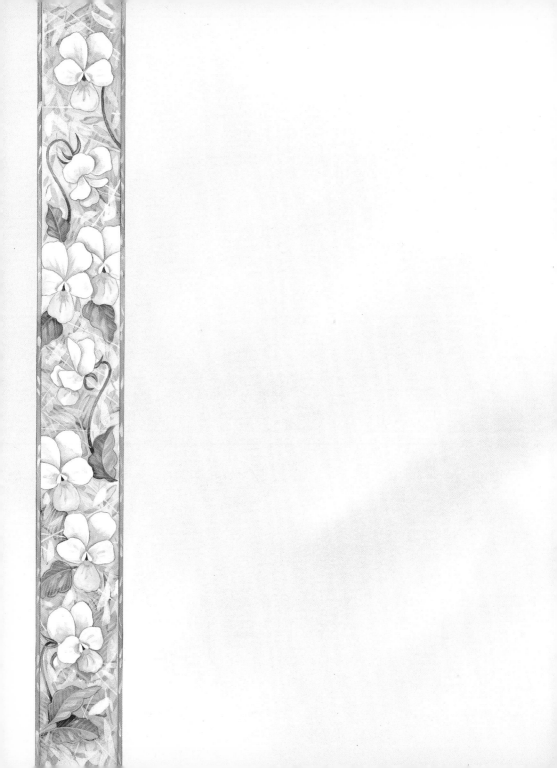

We reject pedestals, queenhood, and walking ten paces behind. To be recognized as human, levelly human, is enough.

Combahee River Collective

Mothering/nurturing is a vital force and process establishing relationships throughout the universe. Exploring and analyzing the nature of all components involved in a nurturing activity puts one in touch with life extending itself. This is the feminine presence. The earth is woman.

Bernice J. Reagon

Women understand the problems of the nation better than men for women have solved the problems of human life from embryo to birth and from birth to maturity. Women are the survival kit of the human race.

Councillor Mandizvidza of Mucheke Township, Zimbabwe, 1983

Women once knew their place – and so do we. Our home is the universe. Our task is anything we set our minds and hearts to.

Maya V. Patel, b.1943